the volunteer's
BACK POCKET
GUIDE TO

sex

GUIDING TEENAGERS ON ISSUES FROM PORNOGRAPHY TO PURITY

BY CRAIG GROSS AND CRIS CLAPP LOGAN

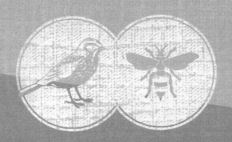

The Volunteer's Back Pocket Guide to Sex
Guiding Teenagers on Issues From Pornography to Purity

Credits
Authors: Craig Gross and Cris Clapp Logan
Executive Developer: Nadim Najm
Chief Creative Officer: Joani Schultz
Copy Editor: Rob Cunningham
Cover Art and Production: Veronica Preston
Production Manager: DeAnne Lear

Unless otherwise indicated, all Scripture quotations are taken from the *Holy Bible*, New Living Translation, copyright © 1996, 2004, 2007. Used by permission of Tyndale House Publishers, Inc., Carol Stream, Illinois 60188. All rights reserved.

ISBN 978-0-7644-7762-1

10 9 8 7 6 5 4 3 2 1   20 19 18 17 16 15 14 13 12

Printed in the United States of America.

CONTENTS

INTRODUCTION

More likely than not, the youth group you volunteer with today looks a whole lot different from the youth group of 10, 20, or 30 years ago. Girls show up wearing tiny miniskirts and clearly visible lacy bras. Guys joke about oral sex with no hint of embarrassment. Many teenagers are hooking up with their friends, their friends' friends, and even their friends' friends' friends (sometimes even at youth group events).

Our teenagers live in a culture where swinging, S&M, and sexting are the norm. Throughout popular media—whether TV shows, video games, or movies—sex has been reduced to skin on skin. For many teenagers, sex has become a purely physical act, fully divorced from spirituality, love, and commitment. Sex, pornography, and "hooking up" are all met with the same response: "It's no big deal."

Most teenagers today don't know where to turn to learn about sex, and many feel confused, fearful, and alone as a result. Those who are struggling with sexual addiction or unhealthy patterns don't know how to find freedom and healing from the choices they've made, and they are afraid the church will label them as perverts if they come clean with their true struggles.

Youth group leaders often ask: "Where are the parents in all of this?!?" Unfortunately, many parents fail to set a Christ-like example. Other parents are simply too terrified or overwhelmed to talk with their teenagers about sex. They think their teenagers are strong enough or good enough to stay "pure," and if they aren't, these parents don't want to know about it. Some parents write off their child's behavior as "kids being kids." In fact, one 15-year-old girl told me (Cris) that her non-Christian parents practically mocked her when she told them of her decision to keep sex until marriage.

The good news is that this means you—the youth worker—are on the front lines of the battle to shape, challenge, and encourage students toward sexual wholeness and purity.

Talking about these topics isn't easy, but this book aims to help. Over the coming pages, we will provide you with practical, down-and-dirty information to help you talk with students on the topics of pornography, sexuality, masturbation, purity, and more. Although we are approaching this from a Christian perspective, this book doesn't focus on Bible teaching. Instead, we try to use God's truth as the backdrop for our approach to this discussion.

As you go through this book and begin to engage in conversations with your students, remember to:

- Listen to where your students are coming from.

- Initiate conversations about sex, healthy sexuality, and sexual struggles.

- Use everyday opportunities to reinforce God's values and goals for sexual health.

- Be sensitive; don't shame or embarrass.

- Be honest about your own story and what God has taught you about sexual purity. Remember, teenagers value authenticity, and your stories can provide powerful fodder for conversations and lessons learned.

- Be informed, frank, and accurate in your response. If you don't know an answer to a question, don't make one up.

- Pray for your students in this area.

- Attend to your own spiritual health through prayer, Christian community, and the study of God's Word—it's hard to lead well when you're running on spiritual fumes.

SEX ABUSE PREVENTION: RULES AND REGULATIONS

We admit, this chapter isn't very fun, but sex abuse prevention is critically important for every youth leader and volunteer to be educated about, both to protect your students and to protect yourself. That's why it's essential to examine these foundational guidelines before going further into our discussion on sex.

UNDERSTAND THE ISSUE

Before you can address child sexual abuse, you must understand the issue. Let's start with a definition: Child sexual abuse includes any sexual act between an adult and a minor, or between two minors, where one exerts power over the other. Forcing, coercing, or persuading a child to engage in any type of sexual act, including sexual contact, exposure to pornography, engaging in sexual behavior, or communications online or over a mobile device (such as sexting) all qualify as crimes punishable by law.[1]

You may think: "This would *never* happen in my church!" Sadly, research indicates that 1 in 4 girls and 1 in 6 boys will be sexually victimized before adulthood.[2] This means it's highly likely that you know a child that has experienced some form of sexual abuse. It's also very likely that you know an abuser. Perpetrators of child sexual abuse look and act like responsible, normal, caring, and thoughtful people, just like you and me. Up to 30-40 percent of child sexual abuse victims are abused by a family member, and 50 percent are abused by someone outside the family whom they know and trust.[3]

Those who sexually abuse children often have multiple victims, so if you suspect that someone is a perpetrator of child sexual abuse, it's critical that you take action. Jesus himself said this: *"If you cause one of these little ones who trusts in me to fall into sin, it would be better for you to have a large millstone tied around your neck and be drowned in the depths of the sea"* *(Matthew 18:6).*

IMPLEMENT PROGRAMS

If your church or youth group doesn't have a child sex abuse prevention curriculum or class, talk to your youth leader about getting one in place. This can help protect you, your students, and the church you care about and serve. Ask people from any congregation that has experienced child sexual abuse, and they will tell you that they wish they had done more to prevent the abuse from occurring in their community.

COMMUNICATION IS KEY

Communicating about child sexual abuse is also vital to fighting and addressing victimization. For the most part, kids often keep their abuse a secret. They feel ashamed, confused, and afraid.

Some of the kids I (Cris) have worked with fear rejection or ridicule if they tell someone, and they aren't always sure whether what they have experienced was wrong or bad. Sometimes, a kid has made a mistake (such as communicating online in a flirtatious manner or agreeing to meet up with an adult for sex), and they think the victimization is their fault. A sexual perpetrator will often use threats and manipulation to keep a teenager quiet.

Complicating the matter further, teenagers can also have strong feelings for their adult perpetrators. In my work with Internet-initiated abuse, victimized girls often describe the adults who abuse them as their "best friends." These individuals work hard to gain trust and affection from their victims. Perpetrators will always affirm their victims and promise romance, adventure, independence, and freedom—essentially saying all of the powerful words that adolescent ears long to hear.

When working with students, watch for teachable moments and opportunities to talk with them about healthy sexuality. Explain what caring, loving sexual relationships look like. Ask them clear and direct questions, and provide them opportunities to share any experiences they have had. One man, now in his 40s (let's call him "Brian"), once shared with me (Cris) about the years of abuse he suffered at the hands of a church staff member. Brian's parents knew the staff member and trusted him completely. On occasion, Brian's parents seemed to notice something was wrong, but they never asked their son clearly enough to evoke a response. There were many times when Brian wanted to tell his parents about the abuse, but his mouth just froze and he was terrified that he had done something wrong. Brian later said, "If they had just asked one time whether anything that man had done with me made me feel uncomfortable, the floodgates would have opened up." The perpetrator was eventually caught and convicted, but not before the damage was done: Authorities later discovered that this "trusted community member" had abused more than 30 boys, ages 9 to 15.

SETTING HEALTHY BOUNDARIES

To minimize the opportunity for child sexual abuse, you should implement a few guidelines. As a general rule, you should eliminate one-on-one time with any minor of the opposite sex. In fact, it's wise to avoid being alone in a private space with any minor you work with, regardless of their gender. This means that whether we are counseling a teenager or just hanging out, we do so in a public area whenever possible. We can talk about matters of the heart at the local Starbucks® just as well as if we were sitting alone in a car.

Also limit the frequency and channels of communication you use with teenagers. Remember, these students may not have the emotional maturity that you do. Spending hours chatting online or texting back and forth can set a confusing precedent. You may also want to consider whether you are online "friends" with the kids you work with and whether they can see your full profile settings. As youth group volunteers and workers, we walk a fine line between friend and mentor. Even though you might be friends with your students, you are still an adult authority figure, and that means you should relate to them in an age-appropriate fashion.

PHYSICAL TOUCH

As a leader and as an adult, you should also be cautious with your use of physical touch. Appropriate physical touch (such as a side hug after an emotional conversation, a shoulder pat to welcome a student that you haven't seen in a while, or a high-five after a youth group competition) can be a powerful, helpful reinforcement for a teenager, but you should always consider a teenager's personal story and past when deciding if any physical touch is appropriate. With students of the opposite sex, keep the hugs "open-face-sandwich-style," if at all, and remember that all forms of physical touch should occur in a visible, public place. Be above reproach—for your sake and theirs.

RECOGNIZE THAT KIDS ARE CONFUSED AND VULNERABLE

Be delicate with teenagers' emotions. Teenagers are vulnerable, with hormones raging and emotions on overdrive. It's easy for teenagers to get the wrong idea from your attempts at friendship. It's natural for the girls and guys in the youth group to have crushes on adult youth group leaders. Focus on group engagement and activities, and encourage your students toward community with one another. If you discover an upset student of the opposite sex at your retreat campground, enlist another student or leader to help you engage with them until you can locate their youth group leader.

IF YOU DO LEARN OF ABUSE

If a student discloses to you that they have been sexually abused, don't overreact. Your reaction will set a powerful precedent for ongoing communication and will impact whether the student continues to open up about it. If you react with suspicion, anger, or disbelief, a student may change the story, feel guilty, or withdraw.

Don't ask leading questions—ask open-ended questions like "What happened next?" Remind them that it's not their fault and it's not right if they have ever been touched sexually or had sexual relationships with a family member or an adult. Thank the student for telling you and let them know you are on their side.

You can't solve this type of problem on your own—you will need to work as a team, getting your youth leader and a professional involved. Legally, you are required to report any reasonable suspicion of child sexual abuse, but also remember that any time we report child abuse, there is a significant risk of exposure to the child's family. By working as a team, you are more likely to best protect the interests of the child and follow the legal requirements and best protocol available.

WHEN THE ABUSER IS ANOTHER TEENAGER

Child sexual abuse isn't always between an adult and a child; kids can also be the perpetrators. You may encounter teenagers trying to hook up on a youth group retreat, sending or receiving "sext" messages, or viewing or sharing pornography in the back of a church bus. Anytime a minor is exposed to sexual content or is pressured to perform sexually by another minor, child-initiated sexual abuse is at play. Set clear guidelines for what is and what isn't appropriate behavior. Also, try to have a leader present with your students at all times. In my experience as a youth group leader, I (Cris) will sometimes even tag along with guys and girls that pair off during youth group activities to try to limit the opportunities for bad behavior—usually much to the chagrin of the young lovers.

Make sure you've established a protocol for addressing sexual situations among the students. This is especially important on overnight retreats. And be sure to clearly communicate these standards and rules to parents, so there will be no surprises if a situation does arise.

CONCLUDING THOUGHTS

Finally, consider hosting a sex abuse prevention, pornography awareness, or online safety night for parents. This will help them better understand your church's policies, along with what you as a leader are confronted with as you work with teenagers.

RESOURCES:

- Sex abuse prevention resources and training: **Darkness to Light:** d2l.org

- For Internet safety resources and training: **Enough Is Enough's Internet Safety 101:** internetsafety101.org

- Pornography awareness and resources: **XXXChurch.com:** xxxchurch.com

CHAPTER 2

BEING AN EXAMPLE

When we talk with youth leaders about purity, pornography, and sex, more often than not, a few leaders take us aside and confess that they are struggling just as much as the students they lead. They feel inadequate to address these topics because they themselves are falling short. Many leaders have questions of their own about what authentic purity looks like.

If this describes you, remember that Jesus chose a band of sinning misfits to spread his truth, and in John's Gospel, Jesus first revealed himself as the Messiah to a thirsty, promiscuous woman at a well (John 4). Christ's love covers all and can cleanse all. We can bring our shame and guilt before God, and God readily, freely forgives us. You don't need to have a perfect scorecard to be a leader for Christ, but God is seeking authenticity and does want to make you free and whole from sexual sin. It's incredibly difficult to lead your students effectively in this area if you are neck deep into a sexual struggle of your own.

IF YOU ARE STRUGGLING

If you are struggling sexually, whether with pornography or with other sexual boundaries, share your struggle with the Lord and with a mentor or trusted friend who can encourage you and challenge you toward discipline. We believe (and God's Word says!) that two are better than one (Ecclesiastes 4:9-12). In this battle, everyone needs accountability.

Make it a priority to meet weekly with an accountability partner or a small group to share, encourage, and challenge one another toward purity. Get that sin out of the dark. Sharing brings healing and transformation. Have people in your life who will ask you the hard questions about exactly where your eyes, mind, hands, or body went—and why. Accountability and honesty in this area will help you develop spiritual maturity and will help you be a more authentic and effective leader for Christ.

Remember, you can't lead well for long if you are running on spiritual fumes. You can only give what you are daily receiving from Christ; it's from the overflow of God's Word and the Holy Spirit in our lives that we can make the strongest impact on the students we are working with. We can only encourage our students to seek accountability when we are seeking accountability ourselves.

THE STANDARD OF A LEADER

Those of us in leadership are called to a higher standard. We are writing this book from the belief that God's Word in this area is living, active, authoritative, and applicable to life today. This means that we believe that sex is meant for marriage between a man and a woman, and that we should strive for God's standard for sex—that is, that we should flee from every hint of sexual immorality (Ephesians 5:3 and 1 Corinthians 6:18).

Remember, you are an example in all areas, including the music you listen to, movies and TV shows you watch, and fashion trends you follow. I (Cris) learned this lesson as a young volunteer leader of a teen Bible study. At the time, I was in a particularly "preppy" season of style, and I wore polos with the collar "popped." I was also really into a particular rap group that was spitting rhymes that may or may not have been edifying. It wasn't long after those first Bible study meetings that almost all of my students started showing up in preppy polos with their collars popped, and two of the girls told me they had just purchased that rap star's album they had heard in my car. It was a terrifying moment of realization, but it really helped me think about what message I was inadvertently sending to the students I led. Likewise, a male leader confessed that he hadn't thought too much about the content in the video games he played until he was confronted by some parents regarding their son's new interest in Grand Theft Auto®.

So as a leader, take an honest look at yourself. Have you separated your sexual life from your spiritual life? Are the shows and movies you watch stirring you sexually? Are you viewing pornography? Are you making sexual compromises? Are you dressing provocatively or letting your mind run wild in sexual fantasy or lust? Someone once said that you can't lead someone where you haven't already been yourself; until you walk in freedom from sexual brokenness, you won't be able to lead students effectively in this area.

Finally, at the risk of being prudish, for women reading this book: Please be considerate in choosing what to wear when you're with your students. It's possible to dress modestly while also sporting a trend that your students will appreciate.

SHARING YOUR STORY

Talking about your story and God's work in your life can help teenagers feel comfortable with sharing their own struggles. If you have a complicated sexual past, God can still use your story to encourage the students you work with to take a better path. If you have been living a disciplined, sacrificial sexual life, then praise God! Your story of purity can help your students know that, with God, living in purity is possible.

Before sharing, check your motives: Don't share to make your students think you're "cool" or for shock value. If you do, you may inadvertently promote some level of sexual permissiveness. Only share your story if your true intention is to establish subject-specific legitimacy and to help strengthen and encourage the students you work with toward Christ. If you share, use discernment and do so in an age-appropriate fashion. Don't minimize or make light of your own past sexual sins. Be thoughtful about how much detail you reveal. Always approach this topic with prayer and ask God for sensitivity regarding what to share and when.

I (Cris) remember sitting at a Starbucks as a 15-year-old with three other girls in my small group and our youth leader. Halfway through our Frappuccinos®, our leader carefully started talking to us—using plenty of humility and humor—about her teenage struggle with masturbation and how it led her on a path toward sexual compromise later in life. I was blown away that she would open up about such a sensitive topic. But as it turned out, three out of the four of us had been struggling with questions and thoughts about that exact issue. As she shared, it helped us to start sharing our own stories and to establish more authentic accountability. Suddenly, struggling with sex wasn't taboo. Reflecting now on that meeting, I believe that conversation was effective only because our leader had taken the time to know us and earn our trust, and also because she was leaning on the Lord to give her discernment about how and when to share with us this particular part of her spiritual journey.

CHAPTER 3
APPROACHING PURITY

At some point, we all have had to grapple (sometimes literally) with where we would draw the physical line before marriage. Some of you may still have questions that can complicate how you address this subject with your students.

The confusion comes partly from the fact that the Bible doesn't lay out with full detail or clarity the ins and outs of the physical limits that should apply to modern dating. The Bible doesn't talk about anal sex, oral sex, or mutual masturbation. (Imagine a sermon on any of those topics!) But the Bible does have plenty to say about avoiding sexual immorality, and God clearly calls us to purity. As Christians, we are called to honor God with our heart, mind, body, and soul (Deuteronomy 6:5) and to avoid even a hint of sexual immorality (Ephesians 5:3), not just sex outside of marriage.

Our culture adds to the confusion. Sex, pornography, and sexual experimentation are commonplace. We live in an "if you've got it, flaunt it" world where immediate gratification, impulse, pleasure, and individualism reign. Most of the students we work with have been spoon-fed a steady diet of these sexual messages, and many have learned about sex from Internet pornography or the misguided cues of their peers or Hollywood celebrities. Teenagers seem to have sex first and date later. In an average conversation with a student, you're likely to hear about parties filled with oral sex, co-ed group sleepovers, and hot tub hookups. Trying to turn the conversation to "God's plan" and "purity" can be pretty challenging, and many leaders walk away from these interactions feeling hopeless, wondering how to talk about sex in a way that's relevant to today's teenagers.

As youth leaders, it's critical that we help lead and encourage the students we work with toward sexual purity. Remember: God's message about sex is compelling and true. God's call for sexual purity is intertwined with the broader questions we address with our students about who created us, why God created us, and what God created us to be and to do.

We were created for intimacy and relationship, and no created being and no physical act can meet that need apart from God. Much of the reason we pursue sex is because we desire closeness and intimacy, and sex helps us feel those things, but the closeness and intimacy that come from sex are fleeting. Ultimate, lasting intimacy, acceptance, closeness, love, relationship, peace, and joy come only from walking with God, not from sexual experience, dating, or even marriage.

WHERE THE CHURCH HAS BEEN UNHELPFUL
Unfortunately, the church has not always done the best job at expressing God's perspective on healthy sex. In most churches, issues like sex, pornography, and chastity aren't even discussed, leaving teenagers with a lot of questions. Although many points

could be made here, we're going to limit the discussion to the four main things we hear from teenagers today regarding God's perspective on our bodies, the definition of sex, the church's silence, and the church's condemnation of those who struggle sexually.

We teach them bodies are bad
Churches often (though usually unintentionally) tell teenagers that their bodies are bad and their sexual desires are wrong. As a result, sexed-up teenagers feel guilty, ashamed, and abnormal. They worry that if they ever told their Christian friends or their youth group leader what was really going on, they would be rejected as perverts. So sin stays in the dark, and teenagers are driven away from the church and God.

We leave them with a list of rules
When we approach purity and sex from a list of rules and a "just say no" approach, our students are left confused. Under a "just say no" approach, many teenagers will develop a laser focus on technical virginity or create their own set of rules regarding what is permissible and acceptable based on peer pressure and their own desire for personal pleasure. It's important that, as the church, we help our students understand that when we talk about things like purity and sex, we aren't just talking about vaginal sex or "technical virginity." We need to affirm God's vision and context for sex, while broadening our conversation about sex to address the so-called gray areas our students are most curious about.

We're silent on subjects that make us uncomfortable, and when we do address them, we forget to talk to the girls, too
Additionally, the church is often silent on the subjects that teenagers are thinking the most about. We don't talk about STDs, "safe sex," condom use, masturbation, technology, or

pornography; as a result, teenagers are trying to figure out these areas of their sexual life on their own. When we talk in vague generalities about purity, teenagers often wonder how far they can go with their boyfriend or girlfriend while still being "pure." If we do address any of these issues, we tend to address only the guys, limiting sexual sin and struggle to a "guy thing." When we do that, we overlook the fact that girls also have sex drives and struggle with pornography, masturbation, and other sexual sins.

We're full of gloom and doom, and we sometimes lie
Finally, the church sometimes uses scare tactics, misconceptions, or outright falsehoods to promote pure behavior. We've heard from teenagers who have been told the following:

- If you masturbate or have premarital sex, God will punish you by making you infertile.

- If you have sex before you are married, you will feel guilty and be filled with regret.

- If you have sex before you are married, your future spouse (and possibly God) will never forgive you.

- If you masturbate, you will get hairy palms or warts on your hands.

I (Cris) have talked with kids who have stopped believing their leaders and God because they were told something about sex that turned out not to be true. Some really enjoyed their first sexual experience and didn't feel lousy after fooling around. Some have masturbated, and, guess what, they don't have hairy palms. Some have walked away from church because they were made to feel shame, guilt, and embarrassment, and guess where they went? Usually back to an unhealthy sexual pattern.

Remember that the God we serve is a God of grace and mercy. God can make all things new. Yes, there are repercussions for sin, but the repercussions are not always immediate, and God often spares us of the consequences we deserve. As leaders, we can embrace the fact that sex and sexual experiences can feel good, right, or fun to our students while also helping them realize that they aren't experiencing God's best. We don't need to lie, add to God's Word, or condemn as we address these issues.

GOD'S MESSAGE ABOUT PURITY

God created sex and sexual experiences for marriage alone. At times, we've probably all wished that we could be a faithful Christian and engage in premarital sex, watch pornography, or push the limits sexually, but these behaviors clearly don't square up with God's vision for sexual intimacy. In the long run, they simply won't prepare our students for the potent, full-bodied, and pure sex God created for them.

Bodies are good

When we talk about purity, we need to help our students understand the powerful, beautiful, and positive message God provides about our bodies and about sexual relationships. The Bible has some pretty graphic, amazing stories about sex and some very affirming things to say about our bodies. Many students don't realize that God made their bodies, and sex, to be good. In the Genesis creation account, God repeatedly exclaimed that what he had created was "good." Indeed, on the sixth day, after creating man and woman—physical bodies and all—God declared creation "very good." Because God created our bodies, we should not abuse our bodies or treat them disrespectfully. Our bodies matter to God. What's more, God designed our bodies to experience sexual pleasure in marriage.

Sex is God's idea in the first place. Erotic love is a key ingredient to marital intimacy, and God actually instructs us to have sex within marriage. Sex, as God designed it, is a very good and pleasurable thing; however, when divorced from God's intended plan, sex is destructive.

Sex is spiritual

It's helpful to remember that sex is spiritual. Sexual intimacy (in any form) binds people together not only physically, but also emotionally and spiritually. It is a beautiful mystery. That's why many people use sex to try to fill a spiritual void. And that's not surprising, since God designed sex to bind a husband and wife together. But sex outside of marriage will not give the same spiritual reward that sex inside marriage will.

Love and relationship, not legalism

Purity is about understanding the totality of God's redeeming love and experiencing the freedom that comes through honoring God in all parts of life, including our sex life. God's message about sex isn't an unjust command; it's good news. When we become a Christian, we die to ourselves. The Holy Spirit makes his home within us, and we have a resource to help us know right from wrong. We can begin to distinguish the real beauty of God's way from the dim reproduction of the world's way.

The challenge for you, as the youth leader, is to affirm the natural sexual desires students have, while encouraging them to channel those desires in the way God intended. How do you do that?

Well, for one, try to avoid a legalistic approach. As we push our students to channel their sexual desires according to God's game plan, it's tempting to reduce sexual purity to a set of rules. Unfortunately (and fortunately), it's not that easy.

Having sex doesn't just mean vaginal sex. So as a leader, don't focus merely on "technical virginity" and intercourse. Fold issues regarding pornography, oral sex, cybersex, and mutual masturbation into your conversations about sexuality and purity. Help your students think about arousing purity and spiritual growth.

The Bible tells us we should avoid every hint of sexual immorality, and God repeatedly urges us to have a pure mind and body. Christ tells us that if we even think lustfully about someone that isn't our spouse, it's as though we've had an affair with that person (Matthew 5:28). Purity is about more than "just saying no," and honoring God sexually is about more than just turning Scripture into a code of conduct. The Christian life is not about legalism; it's about a relationship with God. The students we work with will never succeed in staying pure if we leave them alone with a list of rules.

Rather than focusing on what to do or not to do physically (in other words, "How far is too far?"), encourage your students to think about how they can draw closer to God in all areas of life—including with their bodies. This means teenagers should try to avoid situations that get them revved up sexually. They may want to limit the amount of one-on-one time they spend with their boyfriend or girlfriend, choosing instead to spend more time on group dates. And help them to think about the impact of other physical interactions with the opposite sex. Each student is different. But for many students, even holding hands, giving massages, or kissing can cause their minds and bodies to struggle toward sexual sin. By staying back from the edge, students are more likely to avoid falling off the sexual cliff.

21

SOME FINAL THOUGHTS: VAN GOGH AND SEX

Growing up, Vincent Van Gogh's "Starry Night" was one of my (Cris) favorite works of art. The painting's rolling sky, mystical mountains, swaying cypress trees, and haloed stars speak to an ecstatic vision of earth and heaven as a harmonious continuum. Like many people, I enjoyed reprints of Van Gogh's work. My college roommate and I displayed a poster of the painting in our dorm room. I felt enriched, inspired, and even challenged as an artist by this reproduction, but when I first saw "Starry Night" in person, my entire perspective changed. I could see the cracks in the paint, the plateaus and valleys created by Van Gogh's sometimes-aggressive strokes. I took in the rich smell of the 100-year-old paint. I marveled at the deep colors on the canvas. For the first time, I *really* experienced Van Gogh. It was then that I realized that the vivid colors and texture of "Starry Night" simply could not be captured in a book or on a poster.

Likewise, most of the teenagers we work with think sex or sexual experimentation outside of marriage is pretty great. Premarital sex can be beautiful, inspiring, and moving. However, it falls flat when compared to sex in marriage, as flat as a Van Gogh poster next to the original. Married sex is a dialogue and a foretaste of heaven. Just as mere oil, pigment, bristles, and canvas can create the masterpiece "Starry Night," a sexual act within marriage can become a work of art. In the right context, sex is an intimate conversation—and even a foretaste of the transcendent.

As youth group leaders, we have to help our students understand the power of the real thing. They need to appreciate the beauty that God ultimately desires for their sexual life. We have to help them see that anything short of God's plan, while compelling and perhaps even having glimmers of beauty at times, simply can't compare to the richness of the sexual context God ordained.

Our culture tells us that what we do with our bodies has no significance, but God reminds us that what we do with our bodies has physical, moral, spiritual, and emotional significance. When we allow our bodies and sexuality to be rightly ordered by God's truth, God can use our bodies and sexual life as tools for God's glory.

CHAPTER 4

MEDIA MESSAGES

Mainstream media's depiction of manhood, womanhood, and marriage is a major challenge to our efforts to help our teenagers adopt a Christian sexual ethic. One must look hard to find attractive portrayals of healthy marriages and anything close to committed, monogamous, marital sex. When I (Cris) talk with teenagers, I'm almost always shocked to learn what their parents let them watch. It's not that most parents don't care. I think they just don't realize how graphic today's cable shows, movies, and music videos are, or the powerful impact these negative and misguided messages have on their kids.

THE RESEARCH
A joint study by the Kaiser Family Foundation and Children Now reported that young teenagers ranked entertainment media as their top source for information regarding sexuality and sexual health, meaning that media outrank parents, peers, and mentors as the primary sexual education for kids today.[4] This is exacerbated by the sharp increase in media usage among

teenagers. A recent report revealed that the average child spends more than 75 hours a week consuming entertainment media—the equivalent of nearly two full-time jobs.[5]

Unfortunately, most of this media is pushing our kids toward "sexualization." By definition, sexualization means making a person, group, or thing to be sexual in nature. The American Psychological Association regards a person as being sexualized when:

- A person's value comes only from his or her sexual appeal or sexual behavior, to the exclusion of other characteristics;

- A person is held to a standard that equates physical attractiveness (narrowly defined) with being sexy;

- A person is sexually objectified—that is, made into a thing for others' sexual use, rather than seen as a person with the capacity for independent action and decision making; or

- Sexuality is inappropriately imposed on a person.[6]

Many recent reports have focused on the sexualization of children and teenagers, particularly of girls. One study analyzed the top 25 most-watched programs among kids aged 12-17. This study found that:

- When teenage girls are shown on screen, they are often depicted in a highly sexual or provocative manner;

- Ninety-eight percent of sexual incidents involving teenage female characters occur with partners with whom they do not have any form of committed relationship;

- Teenage girls initiate the vast majority of sexual interactions on screen and are more likely to depict or insinuate sexual acts or activities in programming than adult women; and

- Sixty-seven percent of episodes involving sexualized scenes with teenage girls were comedic in nature, and in about 73 percent of the depictions of sexual scenes, the sexual interactions were presented in a humorous manner—for instance, as a punch line in a joke.[7]

Another recent study of primetime cartoon programming targeted to kids aged 12-17 found that profanity-laden storylines involving themes relating to pornography, rape, cocaine, STDs, and even crystal meth are the "new norm" for teen and tween cartoon programming.[8] As the report highlighted, there were numerous sexual references in animated TV-PG and TV-14 programming:

- They include references to: vagina, penis, pornography, rape, pedophilia, STDs, condoms, virginity, strippers, testicles, breasts, sperm, slang anatomical reference, and general sexual innuendos.

- Sexual content also surpassed every form of violence in animated primetime cable programming. Sexual content included: nudity, emphasizing sexual body parts (such as close-ups of breasts), sexual clothing (including dominatrix outfits, sexy lingerie, and thong panties), suggestive dancing, stripping, simulations of sexual intercourse, pornography, masturbation, pedophilia, and prostitution.

- Forty-three percent of all the sexual incidents were actually depictions rather than references.

- Seventy-four percent of all nudity that aired was on TV-PG animated programming. Only 27 percent of the nudity either was implied or had characters' sexual body parts obscured during the scene. In other words, some form of nudity was depicted on TV-PG programming once every 17 minutes and 50 seconds (equivalent to 3.37 depictions per hour) compared to nudity being depicted on TV-14 programming approximately once every hour.[9]

There have also been several studies examining the increase in all forms of female victimization in storylines—including an increase in the depiction of teenage girls as victims, an increase in the use of female victimization as a punch line in comedy series, and an increase in the depiction of intimate partner violence among teenagers.[10]

RECOGNIZING THE MESSAGES

Soft-porn norm

As a youth leader, your experience is probably consistent with these findings. If you're plugged in to what teenagers are consuming, you've probably noticed that products, movies, music, clothing, and TV shows marketed to teenagers regularly include provocative images and content that the previous generation would have been labeled "soft porn." Watch a few hours of TV shows on so-called family- and teenage-focused networks, and you're bound to encounter lighthearted mentions of pornography and romanticized premarital sex. The top music videos regularly feature crotch grabs, near-naked dancers, stripper-inspired dance moves, S&M references, violence, girl-on-girl action, and even voyeuristic and fetish sex themes. Additionally, the media's depictions of women provide a pathway for pornography use and sexual addiction. Guys are constantly bombarded with scantily clad women. Watch a football game, and what's part of the package? Bikinis and breasts. Flip through a newspaper or sports magazine, and you're bound to come across lingerie ads and provocatively dressed women. Drive down the highway, and you'll undoubtedly encounter erotic billboards. An average movie rated PG-13 or R is filled with sexual innuendo, girls taking their tops off, male and female nudity, simulated sex, and hooking up. The message to men is the more women, the better. It's OK to reduce a woman to her parts—to judge her by her breasts, her butt, her lips, and her legs. Women are objects for pleasure and little else. Sex without commitment, friends with benefits, and sexual experimentation are rites of passage and an essential part of authentic manhood.

Boundless freedom

I (Cris) recently took a day trip with my husband to a beautiful vineyard home in southern Virginia with a group of teenagers, college-aged kids, 20-somethings, married couples, and children. We had a great time swimming in the lake, fishing for bass, and eating barbeque and cupcakes. As the sun finally set, someone turned up the music and a spontaneous dance party broke out on the patio. The song choices spanned every genre and generation—from Motown to country, featuring artists like the Bee Gees, Beyonce, Rihanna, Marvin Gaye, and the B-52s.

At some point, Lady Gaga's song "Born This Way" came on. Just one week earlier, I had been asked to speak to a group of leaders about the content in the song and music video, so I was well-acquainted with the lyrics. The song testifies proudly to the religion of our day: "It doesn't matter if you love him or capital H-I-M/…Don't hide yourself in regret/Just love yourself and you're set/…A different lover is not a sin/…There ain't no other way/Baby I was born this way." According to the song, your priority should be to seek your own personal happiness and fulfill your natural instincts and desires. The way you do it doesn't matter.

As the song's addictive beat pulsed across the yard, a surge of enthusiasm came over all of the tweens and little kids. These 7-, 9-, and 10-year-olds knew every single word. They sang and danced to the song like it was their personal anthem, their victory cry. Like well-trained backup dancers, they mimicked the sexually suggestive dance moves performed by Gaga and her dance troupe in the music video.

How is it possible that these girls, many under 10 years old, have so internalized a song like "Born This Way" that they have memorized its lyrics and choreography? To me, it speaks to the power of media. A whole new generation has been desensitized to sexual, suggestive, and explicit content. And sex sells. As C.S. Lewis wrote many years ago, "We have grown up surrounded by propaganda in favor of unchastity. There are people who want to keep our sex instinct inflamed in order to make money out of us. Because, of course, a man with an obsession is a man who has very little sales resistance."[11]

Our culture and media tell us that there is nothing wrong with our current state of sexual interest and appetite. However, just as a glutton abuses a good thing (food), so we have taken a good thing (sex) and turned it into a monster. Again, Lewis is right on point:

> "You can get a large audience together for a strip-tease act—that is, to watch a girl undress on the stage: now suppose you came to a country where you could fill a theater by simply bringing a covered plate to the stage and then slowly lifting the cover so as to let everyone

see, just before the lights went out, that it contained a mutton chop or a bit of bacon, wouldn't you think that in that country something had gone wrong with the appetite for food? And wouldn't anyone who had grown up in a different world think there was something equally wrong about the state of the sex instinct among us? You find very few people who want to eat things that really aren't food or to do things with food instead of eating it. In other words, perversions of the food appetite are rare. But perversions of the sex instinct are numerous, hard to cure and frightful… you and I, for the last twenty years, have been fed all day long on good solid lies about sex."[12]

The ground is fertile in our culture for shows that celebrate sex without strings, for music videos that look a lot like porn, and for movies that make fun of marriage and disparage married sex. As mentors and youth leaders, we must consider how to make our students fertile soil for God's messages, where they yearn for purity instead of sensuality. We need to help our students realize that the "boundless freedom" Gaga and many other celebrities espouse, with its "pornified" sex and sexualized childhoods, where gender, marriage, and purity don't matter, is no real freedom at all. We must help our students move to a place where God's unfailing love—and God's ultimate truth about marriage, family, and sex—is their personal anthem, a victory cry they actually want to sing.

When marriage starts, sex stops
Depictions of solid marriages and strong, caring parents are also lacking. One young adult recently mentioned a new highly acclaimed cable show she had watched. The first episode of this "must see" hit featured a careless, narcissistic, alcoholic father who provides nothing in the way of parenting or financial support

for his kids. The first show featured oral sex, pornography, explicit sex talk, full male and female nudity, graphic sex, drugs, and S&M. The only passion, love, and sex occur in the context of infatuation and hook-ups.

The message in our media is clear: When marriage starts, sex stops. Families and marriages are a mess, so why bother? You should only marry (if at all) after you've fully discovered yourself and established yourself professionally. Real sexual freedom has no boundaries, place, or rules—sexual fulfillment comes through experimentation and personal satisfaction. What you do with your body doesn't really matter. You can and should pursue every form of sexual pleasure available, because sex outside of marriage has no relational, bodily, or emotional repercussions.

Appearance is everything
You've probably also noticed that the media place a premium on the way we look, especially girls. I (Cris) once asked a group of seventh-grade girls to write down what they thought an ideal woman should be like. Almost all of their answers focused on physical characteristics: blonde, thin, tan, skinny, full lips, big breasts, long legs, shiny hair, flat stomach, sexy, well-dressed. When I asked them whether they would rather be successful, happy, beautiful, sexy, smart, or secure, the vast majority wanted to be sexy or beautiful. Given the "beautiful is better" message that our kids are bombarded with, it is unsurprising that the number of teenagers getting breast implants, rhinoplasties, and Botox® is on the rise.

BEING PROACTIVE
The media are attacking our kids. Several studies report the negative impact that frequent exposure to sexualized media images can cause. Kids with increased exposure, whether

male or female, have higher risks to their cognitive, emotional, and physical development, and they are more likely to struggle with self-image. Further, research shows that girls and young women who consume more mainstream media content are more accepting of stereotypes that depict women as sexual objects; experience higher body dissatisfaction, more depression, and lower self-esteem; and have inaccurate and unhealthy perceptions of virginity and their first sexual experience.[13]

As youth leaders, we need to engage, rather than dismiss or ignore, the media messages teenagers are consuming. We must lead from a place of understanding instead of a place of ignorance.

Discussion is vital. Initiate conversations to help students understand the marketing and commoditization behind the images, videos, and movies they see. Try to keep up with the media content teenagers are absorbing. Help your students to think more about being in the world but not of the world. As Christians, we have God's eyes to see and discern God's truth from the world's lies. Ask strategic questions, such as:

- What do you think of [a certain popular celebrity]?

- What do you think that song is about?

- What does that scene/movie/lyric say about sex and relationships?

- How do the messages in that show/movie/song about sex, love, and relationships compare to God's message about sex, love, and relationships?

- What impact do you think the shows/movies/videos you watch have on you and your friends?

- Are your favorite shows/movies/music beneficial to your walk with God?

With God's help, our students will be able to see past the charade and be thoughtful about the way they interact with the culture.

PORNOGRAPHY

In an ideal world, our students would learn about sex in age-appropriate, incremental stages based on what their parents, educators, and physicians know about healthy child development. Parents would help their kids develop a healthy perspective on relationships, sex, intimacy, love, and marriage, and they would be able to protect them from harmful, explicit, and violent content.

Unfortunately, most parents are clueless, overwhelmed, or intimidated when it comes to talking with their kids about sexuality, much less pornography. And so they turn away as their kids idolize nearly naked pop-princesses, watch "family channel" shows filled with insinuated and simulated premarital sex, and have unrestricted access to pornography through gaming devices, mobile phones, and laptops. As a result, the powerful, misleading messages portrayed in the media and through Internet pornography are taking the lead in educating our students about sex.

PORNOGRAPHY: THE NEW SEX ED

While there are many helpful and age-appropriate sex education sites online, the average student we work with is likely to have had multiple experiences with hard-core pornography by the time they reach their teenage years. The average age at which children will first encounter pornography is 11. However, many clinicians suggest that due to pornography's ubiquity online, first-time exposure is likely to occur at much younger ages in the future. Through the Internet, anyone, including every teenager we work with, has free, easy, and anonymous access to every kind of sexual content.

As one 15-year-old explained to me (Cris), "You don't have to wait for a sex-ed class in school or have a talk with your parents anymore to learn about sex. You can just go online to find everything you need. The Internet and pornography are where most of my friends have learned what to do." A 14-year-old girl shared, "When the guys in my class see something in pornography, they want us to do it. Most of my friends first saw pornography on their dad's computer, or accidentally when they were younger, or with their boyfriends. At first it freaks us out, but then we get used to it. It's just what kids do today. It's no big deal." Another 16-year-old girl confessed, "It can be hard to keep up. I feel like I have to look that way and act that way for guys to think I'm hot. We have to watch that stuff to know what to do."

PORNOGRAPHY: CLEAN, WHOLESOME FUN?

I (Cris) recently came across Cosmopolitan's 2010 Sex Survey, which reported that 36 percent of women use pornography as a "sex enhancer."[14] In another Cosmo article, the magazine implores its readers to explore the many "benefits" of pornography. One paragraph said: "While one must be aware of the dangers of porn addiction, [pornography] can be used as a healthy tool to stimulate one's sex life. Caution: much of the material out there isn't for the fainthearted. But then, Cosmo chicas don't really need that warning, do they?"[15]

While statistics vary wildly regarding the actual percentage of men, women, and children viewing pornography, the theme is consistent: Pornography use has become normalized in our culture. Porn stars are now mainstream icons; little girls wear the Playboy® bunny with pride on their T-shirts; our music industry continues to push the limits of "sexual expression" to the point that today's music videos resemble the "soft-core" pornography of yesterday. As author Gail Dines describes in her book *Pornland*, shows like *Girls Gone Wild* have positioned themselves "not as a porn product, but rather as hot, sexy fun that pushes the envelope of mainstream pop culture."[16]

The accessibility to soft-core pornography, "user-generated" pornography, and TV shows like *Girls Gone Wild* and *Girls Next Door* has filled a gap for the pornography industry where, as Dines explains, "in the place of scripted and carefully crafted scenes of hard-core porn" viewers witness "real" women creating porn and engaging in porn-inspired acts as a "sexy" part of a normal woman's everyday life. Using ordinary women in pornography "socializes users to believe that everyday women are sexually available" and experimental, and emphasizes that a young woman's identity is wrapped up in the fact that she is "a sexual being at the exclusion of anything else." Dines goes on to say that the pornography industry has worked carefully and strategically to "sanitize its products by stripping away the 'dirt' factor and reconstituting porn as normal, healthy, fun, edgy, chic, sexy and hot."[17]

PORNOGRAPHY'S NEW HARD-CORE NORM

Some of you may not get why this is a big deal—although we hope you do! Perhaps you stumbled across a Playboy magazine as a youngster and you don't feel damaged as a result. Perhaps you've only been exposed to soft-core pornography, or maybe you are part of the minority of adults who have never encountered pornography. If so, it's critical to understand that pornography has dramatically changed with the advent of the Internet.

Unfortunately, once users scrape beyond the soft-core surface of the pornography industry, they will dive into the "anything goes" world of hard-core pornography. The explosion of users and pornography sites has challenged the profit-making model of most mainstream pornographers. With so much exposure, people need a new high. So both to differentiate their product and to combat user desensitization, pornography producers have created a vast array of niche, hard-core, violent, and fetish pornography. Many pornography stars have explained that the actions commonly depicted in today's pornography were almost nonexistent before the advent of the Internet. What was once considered hard-core pornography is now considered mainstream.

A quick look at some of the categories offered by one of the top pornography sites today offers an array of niche content. In one analysis of 50 best-selling adult titles, half of the 304 scenes surveyed showed extreme verbal aggression and over 88 percent included extreme physical aggression.[18]

One teenager I (Cris) spoke with told me that just the weekend before, his friend had shown him a "hilarious" video of a woman who was "getting it everywhere from some machines." He continued, "It was insane! It wasn't even, like, so much of a turn-on, as it was just hilarious." Another 14-year-old told me how he really got into anime pornography when he noticed a few cartoon videos on a popular pornography site. "Nothing compares to those cartoon breasts, they're awesome!"

In this context, it really shouldn't be much of a surprise to us that kids are pushing the sexual limits at younger and younger ages. As kids watch this hard-core, fetish-filled porn, their understanding of normal, healthy sexual behavior becomes extremely skewed.

IS PORNOGRAPHY JUST HARMLESS FUN?
Contrary to what the culture says, pornography is not just "harmless fun."

An industry filled with abuse
The pornography industry is filled with victims of physical, emotional, and sexual abuse. Many popular pornography stars have confessed that they were molested as children or that they felt forced into the industry. Lots of women we work with who have come out of the industry talk about the emotional, spiritual, and physical pain they endured as pornography actresses. Many have STDs and have undergone numerous surgeries to keep up with the porn star standard, and some have required surgeries to repair torn orifices.

There are also numerous connections between the sex trafficking world and the pornography industry. It can be very difficult to distinguish between a legal, 18-year-old pornography actress and a 14-year-old who has been forced by her father or pimp to perform on screen. Brothel owners around the world are exploiting 10-, 12-, and 14-year-old girls to turn tricks in their shops and to also generate revenue online. Your students simply can't be sure whether they're watching a "barely legal" adult performing by choice, or a desperate, victimized, exploited young girl performing for her life.

Unhealthy emotional outlet

Looking at pornography can also become an unhealthy outlet for many teenagers and adults. Many teenagers turn to pornography to numb them from pain, embarrassment, or rejection. Some may begin to depend on pornography for sexual release. The patterns that our students establish in their youth will often carry over into their adult life. We have worked with numerous men and women who assumed they could walk away from pornography someday, only to discover that they had developed an emotional dependence on pornography to reach their sexual high.

Desensitization

Many pornography users become desensitized to even hard-core content, and some cross the line into viewing illegal content, even child pornography. One 18-year-old confessed, "I'm so ashamed of what I look at. I never imagined everything that was out there, and what could get me going. I'm almost repulsed by the very content that I get off to. And it's hard not to think about those images and videos, even when I'm with my girlfriend. It's like she just isn't enough for me."

Impact on healthy relationships

A recent report examined a group of young adults—the first generation to grow up with a steady diet of Internet pornography—and found that nearly 9 out of 10 young men (87 percent) and one-third of young women (31 percent) report regular use of pornography. Roughly two-thirds (67 percent) of young men and one-half (49 percent) of young women agreed that pornography use is normal and acceptable behavior.[19] The same study indicated that pornography consumption has serious consequences on marriage, family, and purity. Those who watch pornography are less likely to get married and are more likely to have a high number of sexual partners and to struggle with depression and substance abuse. If they do get married, they are significantly more likely to have affairs and end their marriage in divorce.[20]

A lot of kids think that watching pornography will actually aid them sexually—and this message is prevalent in the media culture. Some health professionals, however, have started to sense that extensive pornography use may be inhibiting men's ability to connect sexually with real human beings. As one lawyer shared with New York Magazine, "I used to race home to have sex with my wife, but now, I leave work a half-hour early so I can get home before she does and masturbate to porn."[21] As musician John Mayer explained to Rolling Stone, "You wake up in the morning, open a thumbnail page, and it leads to a Pandora's box of visuals."[22] And as a mom shared, she and her husband discovered that in just one night of browsing, their pre-teen son had visited more than 800 pornography sites, and now, as a grown adult, he still struggles to be free from his compulsive use of pornography.

Addictive access
Scientists tell us that the prefrontal cortex of the brain, the part of the brain responsible for a person's sense of judgment, reason, emotions, expectations, and maturity, is not fully developed until an individual is in their early to mid-20s. When our students are exposed to this potent material online and through the media, it short-circuits and distorts the normal development process critical to ensuring that teenagers develop in a healthy sexual way. Pornography supplies misinformation about a child's

sexuality, sense of self, and body, and often leads a child down a rabbit hole of harmful content and behaviors.

While there is much debate on whether or not pornography is "addictive," in our line of work, we hear story after story of kids (and parents) exhibiting addictive patterns of behaviors with online pornography. Scientists tend to agree that during an orgasm, a dopamine-oxytocin combination is released in the brain, which behavioral therapists explain helps people have an emotional attachment with the people (or object) they have sex with. What's interesting about pornography and masturbation is that you don't need to have actual sexual intercourse with a real, live human to have an orgasm, but because of the way God designed us, we still have a mental response toward connection. So when you watch porn, you bond with it, and those same chemicals are released, which make you want to come back to repeat that feeling. Some behavioral therapists have explained that this mental-physical-chemical reaction can help us develop a neurological attachment to pornography. This may be one of the reasons why the family therapists I (Cris) talk with are seeing a huge spike in the number of children and teenagers seeking help for sexually addictive behaviors related to pornography use.

ACTION STEPS

Unfortunately, the pornography "fantasy" is spilling over into almost every corner of our culture—pushing powerful messages about human sexuality, sexual relationships, women's bodies, sexual expectations, sexual norms, and how men and women should relate. As one report explained, "Modern trends in pornography consumption and production, sexualized media, sex crime, online sexual predators, Internet dating services, and sexualized cyber-bullying, have created a world more sexually disorienting, daunting, and aggressive than ever before."[23] In this world, our children are exposed to pornographic and sexual content at earlier and earlier ages, in developmentally damaging ways.

Talk about it

Undoubtedly, pornography is an incredibly awkward and difficult subject to talk about with our students, but it's a huge issue that impacts nearly every teenager you work with. The enemy is using pornography to break up marriages, create false expectations, drive people away from authentic love and intimacy, and, of course, create distance between God and God's people. The next generation's sexual health and relational stability are at stake, and no one is immune to being impacted by the onslaught of the culture's sexual messages.

More likely than not, if you've established trust with your students, once you start talking with them about this subject, you won't be able to get them to stop sharing personal stories. Teenagers today are very confused, and they are thirsty for clear answers and help.

Stay calm

Remember to stay calm, use appropriate humor, and approach this subject with humility. Listen to what your students say, and don't condemn or shame them in any way. Don't forget that, for most teenagers, this is the "new norm." It's possible that you will hear about things that will shock and even disgust you, but you can't let that show. Encourage your students to seek God and to share their struggles before God. Although viewing pornography can make them feel distant from God, he is waiting for them to return to him and accept his love and forgiveness.

Speak God's truth

Also, remind them what God has to say. Although the Bible doesn't directly talk about "Internet pornography," the Greek term *pornea* is found throughout the New Testament, and it's the root of our English word *pornography*. And when *pornea* is used, it's talking about sexual sin or sex outside of the marital context God prescribes. Likewise, pornography represents a form of sexual escape and sexual experience outside the marital context for which God created sex.

Additionally, although the Ten Commandments don't say, "Thou shalt not look at pornography," they do tell us we should not commit adultery, and Jesus got to the real meaning of this commandment when he said, *"I say, anyone who even looks at a woman with lust has already committed adultery with her in his heart" (Matthew 5:28).* When our students look at pornography, they are lusting after a man or a woman (or sometimes a group of them together—or even cartoons), and they're committing adultery in their heart and mind. God's Word tells us that our bodies, our minds, and our hearts were not meant for sexual immorality, but for purity, and that we should avoid every hint of sexual immorality—anything that causes our mind, our heart, and our body to sin and lust, and pornography certainly does this.

Help them establish safeguards

As a leader, help your students distinguish God's truth from the lies of the culture. Remind them that you are there to help. If they are struggling with pornography, talk to them about accountability and setting into place practices that can help them avoid situations that get them in trouble. One student stopped taking his mobile device and computer into his room at night, because he knew the temptation would just be too strong. Another student was brave enough to talk with his parents and get them to purchase a filter and accountability software to help him make better choices online. Two teenage girls that were both struggling with using cybersex rooms agreed to meet every week before school to debrief and encourage each other to make Christ-like choices online and to abstain from visiting sites that tempted them to sin.

Pray and lead with sensitivity
Given the gravity of the topic, pray and stay in God's Word to discern when it's right to start talking to your students about this issue. When I (Cris) decided to start addressing this issue with my students, I gave them a heads-up that we were going to talk about sex, purity, and pornography during our next meeting. I also communicated with parents and church leadership so they knew what we were going to discuss. It's imperative that parents and leaders stay in the loop when we address these kinds of topics. At our meeting, I told students about my own early exposure to pornography (without going into the nature of the content), how it made me feel then, and how it impacted my understanding of sexuality later in life. I asked many questions regarding whether they had seen pornography and whether they believed people from school were looking at pornography. I asked how it made them feel when their peers looked at pornography, and I told them about the harms related to viewing pornography.

Confront sin
Some teenagers will probably tell you that they look at pornography so they won't have sex with their girlfriend or boyfriend. Help them to realize that sin is still sin. Rather than establishing their own standards for purity and focusing on what feeds their sexual desires, they need to focus on the behaviors that will help them draw closer to God.

Talk to them about the unhealthy precedent they are setting for the rest of their lives, and help them to better understand the many harms of pornography use. Our students' habituation to pornographic imagery predisposes them to engage in sexually risky behavior. One study found a strong association between pornography consumption and engaging in oral sex and anal sexual intercourse among adolescents.[24]

If your students are looking at pornography, some of them may not understand why this is a big deal. It's possible that their porn use has not affected them significantly yet. Unfortunately, what often begins as occasional use can easily blossom into full-bodied addiction to pornography. Many teenagers believe they will stop using pornography once they get married, but, generally, the practices that we establish during our single years are practices that we bring into our marriage years. In our line of work, we've met thousands of people who have told us that pornography has led them to places and behaviors they wish they had never experienced. While your students may seem to be enjoying a consequence-free season of pornography-related sin, at some point, they will reap what they sow.

CHAPTER
6

BODY IMAGE

As a youth leader, you don't need us to tell you that most teenagers are obsessed with the way they look. And often this revolves around being sexy. Unfortunately, the media's standard for "sexy" is unachievable without surgery, professional makeup teams, and diet pills. As such, many of the students we work with feel as though they are falling short of the sexy standard, generating a lot of insecurity and anxiety. One study reports that by age 13, 53 percent of American girls are unhappy with their bodies.[25] This number grows to 78 percent by the time the girls reach 17.[26]

One would think that people who are unhappy with their bodies would cover them up, rather than expose them. But that's not what's happening. A male youth leader told me that being at high school youth group events felt like walking through a minefield because the girls showed so much skin; he was constantly averting his eyes from revealing bras and camisoles, barely-there miniskirts, thongs and butt cracks coming out of too-tight jeans.

And while guys tend to be less obsessed with their own bodies, many are very insecure about how developed or undeveloped they are sexually—and certainly they are quite focused on the sexiness of the girls around them.

Why the emphasis on outward appearance? And why do our students feel like they have to be sexier?

There's no single answer, but we think a lot of it has to do with their constant intake of sex-obsessed media, advertising, and porn. They are just responding to the culture around them.

Our teenagers are being targeted by consumer advertisers and teen magazines pushing the latest fashions on rail-thin models, many of whom have been surgically altered, digitally manipulated, or air-brushed. A Kaiser Family Foundation study found that more than one in three articles in leading teen girl magazines included a focus on appearance, and most of the advertisements used an appeal to beauty to sell their products.[27] In-depth interviews with girls ages 12 and 13 who were regular readers of teen magazines found that girls used the magazines to formulate their concepts of femininity and relied heavily on articles that featured guys' opinions about how to gain male approval and act in relationships with males.[28] Companies have realized that no consumer is too young and that teenagers are particularly vulnerable to commercials, product placements, and advertisement spreads.

TV and movies have a big effect, too. During a normal week, the average teenager will watch hours of reality TV and absorb numerous highly sexualized teen television shows that push them to focus more and more on the way they look. Several studies have found that the amount of time adolescents spend watching movies, music videos, and television shows is closely associated with their degree of body dissatisfaction and their desire to be thin.

Of course, pornography is also a major factor. Pornography trains kids to view each other as sexual objects. Through the Internet, the average teenage boy will have seen thousands of perfectly tanned, surgically enhanced naked women before he is old enough to drive a car. And with more and more female pornography consumers, even young girls feel pressure to fit the porn-star mold.

THE CONSEQUENCES OF BODY OBSESSION
Our society's obsession with appearance is taking a toll on the students we work with, fueling anxiety, sexual compromises, and eating disorders.

Anxiety and sexual compromises
Many teenagers who focus on their bodies struggle with deep insecurity and anxiety. This is complicated by puberty. Because everyone develops at a different pace, the teenagers who are the first or last to develop are often the most insecure, and insecurity can lead to sexual compromise. As one 13-year-old shared:

> *"I've never felt beautiful. The boys in my class never pay attention to me in the way I want. I'm always their friend and never their girlfriend because I just don't think they think I'm hot enough or even attractive. So I started telling some guys I met online about how I felt. A few of them told me they actually really liked my [profile] picture. I started sending them other photos of me, and some of them wanted some sexier pictures, so I sent some. Before long, we started having cybersex online. I don't*

even know most of the guys I hook up with online, but they all tell me I'm beautiful."

Another female student told me (Cris) that she thought if she had sex with her boyfriend, he would stop commenting so much on how good other girls looked. She found out later that he had been cheating on her. She later described how she felt:

"Hurt, confusion, and loneliness filled me. I felt undesired and ugly. I felt like he cheated on me because I wasn't pretty enough. To try to add some stability to my life, or at least to try to make myself feel better, I dated as many guys as I could, with as little emotional attachment as possible. I wanted to forget how I had trusted someone so much. I thought every guy was a new pursuit, someone I could reel in with my body, use, and throw away to try to fill the emotional void in my life. Unfortunately, the further I pushed the hurt from my mind, the more alone I felt, and the more I needed the approval and words and attention of every guy I could get."

Eating disorders

In addition to anxiety and sexual compromise, an overemphasis on appearance leads many teenagers to develop eating disorders. Over one-half of all teenage girls and nearly one-third of teenage guys use unhealthy weight control behaviors such as skipping meals, fasting, smoking cigarettes, vomiting, and taking laxatives.[29] According to the Center for Mental Health Services, females between ages 12 and 25 make up about 90 percent of those who struggle with eating disorders.[30]

The two most common eating disorders are anorexia and bulimia. But other eating disorders—like binge eating, food phobias, and extreme obsession with certain body parts (such as a nose or thighs)—are also becoming more common.

Teenagers who are anorexic often have an intense fear of being overweight. Many anorexic teenagers believe they are fat, regardless of how skinny they actually are. They often weigh food before eating it or compulsively count calories. They may eat only certain foods, weigh themselves repeatedly, or exercise excessively. Because anorexia is a mental disorder, teenagers who struggle with anorexia are often immune to people telling them that they are not fat.

People who are bulimic will often restrict what they eat in public, but binge in private. After eating, they will withdraw to a bathroom to "purge" (throw up) the food they've consumed. They may also use laxatives, diuretics, or enemas. Like people who struggle with anorexia, bulimic teenagers may overexercise to work off the calories from their binges.

Eating disorders are curable, but usually professional help is needed. Eating disorders tend to be associated with a mental imbalance of some sort. If you suspect one of your students is struggling with an eating disorder, talk to your youth group leader or pastor about finding a Christian counselor who specializes in this area.

What about the guys?
Body-related issues aren't limited to girls. Although guys are less likely to talk about their insecurities, the reality is that many guys spend plenty of time thinking about how they look. As noted already, some guys struggle with eating disorders. Many struggle with anxiety. Especially during puberty, a guy's entire self-image can be based on how his body looks and performs. If a guy is ahead of or behind the rest of the pack—for example,

being the only guy with body hair or the first with a squeaky voice (or the only one who isn't going through those changes)— he will probably feel some level of insecurity until things level out.

Society is also putting a lot of pressure on guys to look and act a certain way. Each week welcomes the arrival of new lines of anti-aging moisturizers for men and other male grooming and beauty products. In magazines, male models and celebrities are often just as airbrushed and computer-doctored as female models and celebrities.

Pornography use can make things even more difficult for guys. Their bodies simply don't look like the porn stars they've seen. They feel anxious about whether their penises are large enough or whether they will be able to perform sexually in the same way as porn stars. And as we've discussed in previous chapters, porn exposure also causes many male students to pressure girls to live up to a porn-star standard.

WHAT YOU CAN DO

Help them distinguish fantasy from reality
As you communicate with your students, remind them that almost all teenagers (and most adults!) are self-conscious about their bodies. Almost everyone, even supermodels and celebrities, would like to change a thing or two. Help your students realize that the photos and videos they see are often heavily airbrushed and that the lighting, clothing, makeup, hair, and camera angles are maximized to catch actresses and models at their best.

Help them understand how God sees them

Also help your students identify and vocalize the things about themselves that they value. Encourage your students to have their needs met by their creator and to read and study Scripture about who God created them to be. Remind your students that they are fearfully and wonderfully made (Psalm 139:14). They need to replace the media's priorities and their own negative perspective of themselves with God's truth.

Remind your female students of 1 Peter 3:3-5, which declares that true beauty does not come from the clothes they wear, their hairstyle, their jewelry, or their makeup, but rather from the unfading beauty of leading a life after God's own heart. Challenge your students to think about whether they are putting as much effort into their inner selves as their outer appearance.

Especially for girls, focus on the inner qualities that make them beautiful

When I (Cris) first started working with youth, many of my initial comments to the girls I led were surface-level, often about some article of clothing they were wearing. I greeted them with "you look so pretty today" or "nice boots." While these compliments have their place, if not checked they can send the wrong message. So I started trying to affirm their inner beauty, interests, and growth in the Lord, pushing past the superficial. One of my girls later told me how much it meant to hear words that spoke to her heart, rather than words that just fed her shopping habit.

Help them have perspective

As I (Cris) have counseled girls about their insecurities, I've tried to remind them that often the things they are most uncomfortable about are things that others don't even notice. One very trim, athletic 14-year-old was especially concerned that her stomach stuck out (it didn't). I encouraged her to replace every thought she had about her stomach with a Scripture verse or a blessing that God had given her. At first, the exercise seemed silly to her, but over time, she thought less about her stomach and learned more about walking in the confidence that comes from knowing and following Christ.

Remember the power of words

Words are incredibly powerful, especially to 15-year-olds who are insecure about how they look. So be careful with what you say. When a group of teenage guys laugh at the kid whose voice squeaks at random times, or when a teenage girl tells you that she's concerned that her breasts aren't big enough yet, consider the opportunity in front of you. Will you use your words to build up or to tear down? As the authority figure, your words will stick with them for a long time.

Tackling the porn star standard

Additionally, as you talk with your teenagers about sexuality and pornography, it may be appropriate to discuss the "porn star standard." With girls in particular, explore their worries and concerns about performing like a porn star or measuring up to the surgically enhanced bodies all over the Internet. We have talked with many girls who confessed their worries about not being able to compete with the women their boyfriends look at online.

This type of insecurity can often lead a girl to start watching pornography herself in order to learn porn-star techniques, or to push boundaries with clothing and sexual experimentation. I (Cris) often have to remind my students that the only way any of us can overcome insecurity and fear is by choosing to believe God's words to us. Together with your students, spend time praying that the Lord would strengthen them in their faith and that they would obey God's call on their lives, including with their bodies. We all need to trust in God for our security and affirmation, not in our boyfriends or girlfriends (or even husbands or wives).

Getting help
Sometimes a student's low self-esteem and body image problems are too much to handle alone. As teenagers struggle with body image issues or sexual addictions, they may become depressed, lose interest in activities or friends, resort to alcohol or drug abuse, or even hurt themselves through cutting and self-mutilation. If a student shows any of these symptoms, it may be helpful to talk to him or her about getting a guidance counselor or therapist involved.

SOME CONCLUDING THOUGHTS
God made us as physical beings, and the body is intrinsically a good thing. But our culture's obsession with outward appearance is dangerous and out of step with what God says. As a youth worker, you have a critical role to play in moving students, both guys and girls, toward a healthy understanding of their bodies.

So when you overhear male students commenting on the looks, shapes, and sizes of the women around them, speak up. When your teenage girls go on and on about the latest fashions, say something constructive. While our culture has trained teenagers to focus on the exterior, as Christians we are called to look deeper. It's our responsibility to encourage our students to see themselves and others as individuals made in God's image, not sex objects.

CHAPTER
7

MASTURBATION

No one really wants to talk about masturbation, but just because we don't want to talk about it doesn't mean we shouldn't. Teenagers have lots of questions about this issue. They want to know what God has to say about masturbation, and they probably also want to know what you think about it. And don't assume this is just an issue for the guys; both guys and girls struggle with masturbation. Teenagers tell us that they learned to masturbate from TV shows, movies, Internet pornography, magazines, and even their sex-ed class at school. Most of these sources promote masturbation and self-pleasure as normal, healthy sexual activities that every teenager should engage in.

We realize that opinions about masturbation vary widely in Christian circles. But our perspective is that masturbation is a sin. There, we said it.

This may seem extreme to some, but we've thought a lot about the issue, and we've come to the conclusion that masturbation simply doesn't honor God. Although there isn't any definitive

Scripture verse that says, "Thou shalt not masturbate," God calls us to purity and holiness. With that as a guide, it's clear to us that masturbation is not the type of sexual activity that God created us for. Here are a few reasons why we think teenagers (and the rest of us!) should avoid masturbation.

Masturbation often involves fantasy and lust

First, it's incredibly difficult to honor God while masturbating. Masturbation often involves sexual thoughts, fantasy, and the use of pornography or other sexual media. It's nearly impossible to masturbate without lusting. Jesus told us that if we even look lustfully at someone who is not our spouse, it's as if we have committed adultery.

Masturbation distances us from God

Masturbation tends to make us feel distant from God. Although masturbation feels good in the moment, most of us feel guilty and ashamed about our actions later, and we have a hard time drawing near to God when we feel unclean. And as we continually sin, we begin to numb ourselves from the work of the Holy Spirit. As Christians, we want to walk in a way that honors God. Masturbation doesn't honor God; rather, it hurts our relationship with God.

Masturbation becomes a form of escape

Many people masturbate to numb pain, escape reality, or fill some void relating to insecurity or loneliness. Unfortunately, the intimacy or escape that comes from masturbation never lasts and often drives us further away from God and others. We need to seek real, lasting intimacy with God, not the temporary intimacy that comes with orgasms.

Masturbation teaches us to have selfish sex

Masturbation also teaches us that we don't need anyone else to have a sexual experience. While God created sex to be a unifying, bonding, demonstrative, and sacrificial expression of love between a husband and wife, masturbation teaches us to have sex with ourselves to fulfill our own desires. A lot of teenagers think that when they get married they will be able to stop, but the habit of masturbation can carry well into marriage. We've talked with both men and women who are frustrated that their spouse can't satisfy them sexually as well as they can satisfy themselves, because they're accustomed to masturbation rather than marital sex. Is this really something you want to have to deal with in marriage? Sex with your spouse is hard, but the physical, emotional, and spiritual rewards are tremendous; sex with yourself is easy, but it leads nowhere.

SLIDING SIN SCALE

Many teenagers argue that they need to masturbate so they won't have sex. Usually, however, masturbation intensifies rather than diminishes our sexual desires. Since masturbation isn't the full-bodied sex that God designed us for, it can never fully satisfy our sexual desires and often sets us up for further sin. And when we are willing to make sexual compromises when we are all by ourselves, it becomes even more difficult for us to be disciplined when we are alone with a boyfriend or girlfriend.

HELPING YOUR STUDENTS

As we grow as Christians, we must seek self-discipline and purity. It's part of the Christian life. When it comes to masturbation, we need to encourage our students to choose God's best rather than to take the easy way out. This is all the more important when we consider that the patterns we establish as teenagers—including with sex—will often carry through the rest of our lives.

Unfortunately, pretty much everyone stumbles in this area. It's important to help your students recognize that they are not gross, weird, or perverted for engaging in masturbation. We are all human beings with natural sexual desires. Although masturbation distances us from God, God is waiting for us to return to him. God really doesn't care about how unworthy or unclean we feel. God wants us to allow him to clean us up.

With God's grace as motivation, help your students think about how they can be pure. Ask them to consider how they are feeling when they are most tempted to masturbate. What were the inputs that fueled their lust and sexual tension? Were they alone with their computer late at night? Did they spend time looking at pornography or other sexual content? Did they start fantasizing about a guy or girl in their class? Push them to think carefully about what they see, watch, listen to, and dwell on, which will help them make better choices going forward. And encourage them to join an accountability group and to talk openly with an accountability partner about taking proactive steps to walk in freedom and discipline. Remind them that as Christians, we have access to God's power to help us overcome our struggles, even with an issue as tough as masturbation. As we celebrate small victories, God will reorient our desires and strengthen us in the Spirit to walk in freedom.

XXXchurch.com OPERATION: SAVE THE KITTENS
Did you know that every time you masturbate, God kills a kitten? If your students are familiar with our work at XXXchurch.com, chances are that they have heard about this campaign.

A few years ago, we received a hilarious email from an anonymous person that referred to masturbation as "kitten killing." Since talking about masturbation can undoubtedly be awkward and embarrassing—especially when using the actual "M" word—we launched "Operation Save the Kittens" (OSTK) to provide a strategy for teenagers to talk about their serious struggles in a way that wouldn't raise too many eyebrows at the local coffee shop.

We have encouraged teenagers across the country to get together with their small groups or accountability partners to see how their personal efforts are going to save little innocent kittens. Some of the students that we work with send weekly emails to their friends asking them if they "killed any kittens" that week or reminding one another to "please think of the kittens." Campaigns like OSTK can help our students laugh, share, and be vulnerable with one another while also putting their creative energy toward something that can help them pursue purity. You can find out more about our campaign online at xxxchurch.com/getinvolved/pornpatrol/kittens.html.

CHAPTER
8
HOT-BUTTON
ISSUES

Today's teenagers are confused about sex. They have many questions about sex, pornography, and establishing healthy sexual boundaries. Unfortunately, it's hard to find straight answers in most churches, and many parents aren't setting a strong example or helping their children wade through our "pornified" culture. This means that, as youth leaders, we have our work cut out for us. In this chapter, we aim to address some of the common questions and hot-button issues that we haven't already covered in detail.

As you approach these topics, remember that many teenagers are embarrassed to ask adults for real answers about sex. They don't want to appear clueless, naïve, or stupid. You'll need to invest in getting to know your students and earning their trust before you can safely initiate conversations on this stuff. Watch out for teachable moments to talk about sex and purity. When your students do open up, try not to judge or overreact. Your trust level with the students, and how you react initially, will be the major factors that determine how much you can help a student with these issues.

HOW FAR IS TOO FAR?

This is one of the most common questions we get from teenagers. Unfortunately, it's the wrong question. As Christians, we are called to honor God with our mind, body, and soul. We are to avoid every hint of sexual immorality (Ephesians 5:3), not just intercourse outside of marriage. When you get this question, ask your students first to think through whether their actions honor God. Are they seeking their own personal pleasure or trying to impress or please a peer, or are they seeking to obey God?

Legalistic rules will not keep your students pure. We've all heard the "slippery slope" argument from our parents or pastor: First you're holding hands, then you're embracing, then you're "necking" (whatever that is), and before you know it, you're having sex. That's not what we're saying. Rather than focusing on "how far is too far," help your teenagers focus on honoring God.

That's not to say that boundaries are bad. In fact, boundaries can be helpful. It's not legalism for your students to agree with their boyfriend or girlfriend that they won't use their tongue in any way, if they feel that doing so is likely to be unhelpful in their quest to honor God with their body. But physical boundaries, no matter how firm, can't replace the heart. If your students' hearts are not right, they can forget about holding the line physically. For example, if your students decide not to kiss on the mouth, but their hearts aren't in the right place, then they likely will end up kissing everywhere else and going further than they would have if they were just kissing on the mouth.

I (Cris) often ask my students what they want their marriage life to look like and what sort of sexual baggage they want to bring into marriage. Do they want to have to tell their future spouse how they got STDs? Or how many sexual partners they've had? Do they want to be compared to past lovers? Or struggle with comparing their spouse to the bodies they've seen and the sexual experiences they've had? If our teenagers think through what happens later, they're more likely to make wiser choices about their sexual behavior now.

Even if our students have established physical boundaries, keeping to them is hard. So we need to help them think about which situations are most likely to result in a breached boundary. For example, sitting in a car at night with a boyfriend or girlfriend probably isn't the best way to maintain purity. God exhorts us to flee from sexual temptation (1 Corinthians 6:18). And remember how Joseph ran away from Potiphar's wife in Genesis 39? I was so proud of one of my students who told me that, in the middle of his favorite movie with his girlfriend, he felt so tempted that he hopped up and demanded that they go to a local diner instead, because he could sense his mind and body starting to go on overdrive just from sitting next to her in a dark room. That guy deserved a medal!

Every person is different, susceptible to different levels and types of temptation. For some, it may be wise to avoid physical contact altogether. Even things as innocent as holding hands, giving massages, or kissing can cause minds and bodies to struggle toward sexual sin. Again, the guiding principle is not "How far is too far?" but rather "How can I glorify God the most with my body?"

IS ANAL SEX REALLY SEX?

Ten years ago, most teenagers would not have known what anal sex even was. Those who did know about it probably would not have considered engaging in it. But online pornography—the sex-ed resource for so many of our students—has normalized anal sex. We've talked with countless girls whose boyfriends have asked them if they would "do anal."

It's important to help our students realize that outside of marriage, anal sex isn't normal or healthy. And it's debatable whether anal sex represents God's best even within marriage. Anal sex is not only incredibly intimate, but it is also incredibly risky and (in our view) degrading, and it also is an easy way to spread STDs (despite what some students believe).

Girls should never feel pressured by their boyfriends to experiment with anal sex. Guys should not pressure their girlfriends to engage in this type of behavior. Anal sex is not a safe alternative to "going all the way." Whether inside or outside of marriage, activities that make someone feel degraded, abused, or scared are not part of a loving relationship. Remind your students that just because they aren't engaging in vaginal intercourse doesn't mean they are honoring God's standard for sexual purity.

WHAT ABOUT ORAL SEX?

Our students generally learn about oral sex from their peers, movies, pornography, or TV shows, and many are confused regarding what oral sex actually is. Teenagers (and the culture) use a lot of slang regarding oral sex, which only adds to the confusion. If you're talking with a student about oral sex, it's good to ask them exactly what they are talking about to make sure you are on the same page.

Many teenagers want to know whether oral sex is actually sex and whether they are still virgins if they have had oral sex. While oral sex may not cause one to lose their technical virginity, it will cause them to lose their technical purity. Oral sex is a form of sexual interaction that should be reserved for a man and a woman in marriage. It is an incredibly intimate act of service and pleasure for a husband and wife, alone. People who are seeking to honor God with their bodies and sexuality will pursue the heart and intent of God's law, not just the letter of God's law.

Ask your students if they really want to have to tell their future husband or wife that they "only" had oral sex, not "real" sex. Ask any married Christian person how they felt when they learned their spouse had oral sex with someone else, and chances are that they were hurt, sad, disappointed, or angry to learn that their spouse did it.

Additionally, many teenagers don't realize that they are still at risk of acquiring STDs or even HIV when they perform or receive oral sex. One study from the New England Journal of Medicine concluded that people with one to five oral sex partners in their lifetime had a doubled risk of throat cancer relating to human papillomavirus (commonly known as HPV) as compared to those who never engaged in oral sex, and those with more than five oral sex partners had a 250 percent increased risk.

HOW CAN I GET STDS?
Sexually transmitted diseases (STDs) are infectious diseases that can spread through any type of sexual physical contact between two people. STDs affect girls and guys, regardless of age, race, background, and sexual orientation. STDs have become very common among teenagers. Our culture tends to make light of STDs, and often teenagers view them as more of

an inconvenience or embarrassment, rather than as a big health risk. It's important that we help our students recognize that STDs are actually very serious health problems that, if left untreated, can cause permanent damage, such as infertility, cancer, and even death.

Many teenagers think they can only get STDs if they have vaginal sexual intercourse. The truth is that anyone can get STDs through skin-to-skin contact with an infected area or an open sore. And you can acquire STDs from both anal and oral sex. The bacteria and viruses that cause STDs can enter the body through any tiny cuts or tears in the mouth, anus, penis, or vaginal wall. (Often these slight tears are so small you might not recognize or even see them.)

It's very difficult to tell whether someone has STDs or a related infection that could put others at risk. Many people with STDs don't even know that they have them because these diseases present themselves differently in each individual and can appear dormant in some. These people are at risk of passing on this infection to anyone they have sexual interactions with, regardless of whether they show signs of "breaking out" or infection.

Statistics from the Centers for Disease Control and Prevention (cdc.gov) have shown that the earlier in life a person begins experimenting sexually, the greater his or her chance will be of becoming infected with an STD. People who have more than one sexual partner over their lifetime are much more likely to acquire an STD. Using birth control, like the pill, spermicides, or diaphragms, does not protect a person against STDs, and latex condoms are only partially protective. Rinsing with water or using homemade protection (we've heard of everything from socks to cling wrap!) will not protect an individual from acquiring

STDs or from getting pregnant. Advise your student that if there is any risk that they have an STD, they should get tested immediately and abstain from further sexual activity.

CAN I GET PREGNANT WHEN...?

There's a ton of misinformation out there about when a woman can become pregnant. One that we hear a lot is that it's impossible for a girl to become pregnant the first time she has sex. That's ridiculous. Kids should know that any time a girl has vaginal sex with a guy, regardless of whether it's her first time or if she's on her period, she is at risk of becoming pregnant. Even if a young woman has never menstruated, she may have just ovulated (released an egg) for the first time, which would make pregnancy possible.

Here are some other myths. Instead of condoms, some kids use socks and other articles of clothing, cling wrap, and douching. Of course, clothing is porous and is not a barrier against pregnancy. Rinsing with water (or any other liquid) also does not significantly reduce a girl's chances of becoming pregnant. Even if a guy ejaculates outside of her but near a girl's vagina, pregnancy is possible. If he pulls out before orgasm, she can become pregnant, because semen leaks from the penis even before ejaculation.

Remind your students that even using a condom or being on the pill is not 100 percent guaranteed to prevent pregnancy. (Guys often ask us whether they should "double up" with condoms, but the friction created between the two condoms actually increases the chance that the condoms will break.) The only foolproof way to prevent pregnancy (and all STDs) is to abstain from all types of sex, including oral, vaginal, and anal sex, period.

ARE SEX TOYS OK?

Using pornography, sex toys, and anything else to remain a "technical virgin" is less than God's best. Tell your students that if they are regularly learning about sexual experiences from pleasing themselves with a sex toy, they may have a more difficult time enjoying sex with a real partner. (See the earlier chapter on masturbation.)

IS IT OK TO PIERCE MY TONGUE, NIPPLES, OR GENITALS?

If you get a question like this, just ask why the student wants the piercing. Usually, these types of piercings are done to increase sexual arousal or pleasure. Until your students are married, they won't really know what their spouse is into and whether a piercing will be a turn-on. So we think it's best to tell students to wait until they are married to get their unmentionables pierced.

WHAT IF WE'RE NOT SEXUALLY COMPATIBLE?

We need to help our students realize that sex doesn't really look like it does in the movies. Generally, the first time people have sex, it isn't perfect, regardless of their "compatibility" or "chemistry." One of the wonderful gifts God gives us through married sex is the opportunity to explore, learn, and experiment sexually with each other. The best-case scenario is that a student and their future spouse will be able to learn about sex together, free from comparison, baggage, STDs, and any past regret.

MY BOYFRIEND/GIRLFRIEND TOLD ME THAT HE/SHE WOULD BREAK UP WITH ME IF WE DIDN'T HAVE SEX. WHAT SHOULD I DO?

We can't deny the strong and stormy feelings teenagers experience in high school. The idea of losing the other person can make any teenager feel like they will die. We need to encourage our students to surrender their relationships to the Lord and help them to realize that the right person will wait. It's ultimately up to them: Do they want to honor God or have sex with their boyfriend or girlfriend? Someone who honors God will want to help a boyfriend or girlfriend remain pure, blameless, safe, and respected. Demanding sex is manipulative and out of step with God's plan.

I WANT TO STOP SINNING SEXUALLY, BUT I CAN'T. HELP!

Being holy is hard. But ultimately, the choice is up to us. When we repeatedly choose to serve our own selfish desires or sexual impulses, we will hurt our relationship with God and distance ourselves from experiencing the true love, joy, and peace God wants for us. St. Augustine famously recalled praying as a youth, "Give me chastity...but not yet." Our students need to decide whether or not they are serious about their purity.

If students are serious, then they need to have friends to whom they are accountable, who will ask them the hard questions. Prayer, although critical, is not enough. Our students also need community. As youth leaders, we need to speak God's truth in love to our students and encourage them to do likewise with their friends.

SEXTING AND CYBERSEX

When you combine teenage hormones, impulsivity, and perceived invincibility with our students' easy access to each other, pornography, and technology, the result can be lethal. Our students are persistently bombarded with the message that their worth and value rests in how sexy they look. They are continually encouraged to push the sexual envelope. Ending a sexual experience has become as simple as closing out of a chat room, blocking a user, or shutting down a computer.

In a world where most teenagers have seen pornography or other sexually suggestive and explicit content, is it any surprise that they are emulating what they see?

As one report found:

- As many as 20 percent of teenagers have seen, sent, or received a "sext" message.

- Although most teenagers who send sexually suggestive content are sending it to boyfriends or girlfriends, others say they are sending such material to those they want to hook up with or even to someone they only know online, as a way of "flirting."

- Teenagers are conflicted about sending and posting sexually suggestive content—they know it's potentially dangerous, yet many do it anyway.

- Teenagers who receive nude/semi-nude images and sexually suggestive texts and emails are sharing them with other people for whom they were never intended.[31]

As you engage with your students on these issues, remind them that purity involves more than what we do with our bodies or through physical contact in the offline world. Purity means honoring God in the private and public, the online and offline moments of life, with our full heart, mind, soul, and body. Just because your students aren't crossing any physical boundaries offline doesn't mean they necessarily are honoring God. When they engage in cybersex, they are lusting and connecting sexually with someone that isn't their husband or wife. The images and chat sessions will shape and form their sexual appetites and behaviors well into their adult life.

Additionally, it can be very difficult to know the real identities and motives of the people your students meet online. Many of the people engaged in cybersex are not really who they say they are. We've worked with guys and girls who have learned that the person they were sharing so much of themselves with online was a far cry from whom they represented themselves to be. The person on the other side of the screen could be married and have a family, and chances are they have no intention of being an offline boyfriend or girlfriend to the teenagers they connect with online.

When our students go online for love, attention, and affirmation rather than to God, they also open themselves up to a world filled with destructive forms of sexual expression. I (Cris) recently spoke with a girl who shared that she went online because the men online told her all of the things she desperately wanted to hear: that she was beautiful, sexy, and thin. She started having an online relationship with one of them, and gradually their chats became more and more sexual. The man she was communicating with started asking her to allow him to make videos of her masturbating, but when she wanted to stop, he threatened to send her parents some of the naked photos he had of her. This particular student continued to travel down a dangerous path, even being coerced to post videos and engage in cybersex on a user-generated pornography site.

73

The fantasy of cyberspace allows people to deceive one another into believing they are someone else. Remind your students that they need to act the same way online that they would at their youth group meetings. Talk to them about what they are doing online, and outline the risks. Talk to them about the consequences, embarrassment, and longevity regarding content and images posted online. Once an image is posted online, it can never be erased. Tell the teenager you work with to think before they post and text. The words, images, and videos they post or text can, and most likely *will*, be seen by someone other than the intended recipient.

ENDNOTES

1. John E.B. Myers, Lucy Berliner, John Briere, C. Terry Hendrix, Theresa Reid, Carole Jenny, editors, *The APSAC Handbook of Child Maltreatment, Second Edition* (Thousand Oaks, CA: Sage Publications, 2002), 55.

2. S.R. Dube, R.F. Anda, C.L. Whitfield, D.W. Brown, V.J. Felitti, M. Dong, W.H. Giles, National Center for Chronic Disease Prevention and Health Promotion (Atlanta, GA: Centers for Disease Control and Prevention).

3. H.N. Synder, "Sexual Assault of Young Children as Reported to Law Enforcement: Victim, Incident and Offender Characteristics," in an NIBRS Statistical Report (Washington, DC: U.S. Department of Justice, 2000).

4. Kaiser Family Foundation and Children Now, "Talking With Kids About Tough Issues: A National Survey of Parents and Kids" (2001). Retrieved from kff.org/mediapartnerships/upload/Talking-With-Kids-About-Tough-Issues-A-National-Survey-of-Parents-and-Kids-Chart-Pack-2.pdf.

5. Kaiser Family Foundation, "Generation M2: Media in the Lives of 8- to 18-Year-Olds" (2010).

6. American Psychological Association Task Force on the Sexualization of Girls, "Report of the APA Task Force on the Sexualization of Girls" (2010). Retrieved from apa.org/pi/women/programs/girls/report-full.pdf.

7. Parents Television Council, "Sexualized Girls: Tinsel Town's New Target, A Study of Teen Female Sexualization" (2010). Retrieved from parentstv.org/FemaleSexualization/Study/Sexualized_Teen_Girls.pdf.

8. Parents Television Council, "Cartoons are No Laughing Matter: Sex, Drugs and Profanity on Primetime Animated Programs" (2011). Retrieved from parentstv.org/PTC/ publications/reports/animation/Report.pdf.

9. Ibid.

10. Parents Television Council, "Women in Peril: A Look at TV's Disturbing New Storyline Trend" (2009). Retrieved from parentstv.org/PTC/publications/reports/womeninperil/study. pdf.

11. C.S. Lewis, *Mere Christianity* (New York, NY: Macmillan Publishing Company, 1960), 93.

12. Ibid, 90-91.

13. American Psychological Association Task Force on the Sexualization of Girls, "Report of the APA Task Force on the Sexualization of Girls" (2010). Retrieved from apa.org/pi/ women/programs/girls/report-full.pdf.

14. "Cosmopolitan Online Sex Survey Results 2010," Cosmopolitan. Retrieved September 17, 2011, from cosmopolitan.co.za/Sex/Stories/cosmopolitan-online-sex-survey-results-2010-danger.

15. "The Cosmo Girl's Guide to Pornography," Cosmopolitan. Retrieved September 18, 2011, from cosmo.intoday.in/ cosmopolitan/story.jsp?sid=7627&page=2.

16. Gail Dines, *Pornland* (Boston, MA: Beacon Press, 2010).

17. Ibid.

18. R. J. Wosnitzer and A. J. Bridges, "Aggression and Sexual Behavior in Best-Selling Pornography: A Content Analysis Update" (2007). Paper presented at the 57th Annual Meeting

of the International Communication Association, San Francisco, California.

19. J. S. Carroll, L. M. Padilla-Walker, L. J. Nelson, C. D. Olson, C. M. Barry, and S. D. Madsen, "Generation XXX: Pornography Acceptance and Use Among Emerging Adults," Journal of Adolescent Research 23, No. 1 (2008), 6-30.

20. Ibid.

21. Davy Rothbart, "He's Just Not That Into Anyone." New York Magazine (January 30, 2011). Retrieved from nymag.com/news/features/70976/.

22. "John Mayer's Dirty Mind & Lonely Heart." Rolling Stone Magazine (January 19, 2010). Retrieved from rollingstone.com/music/news/john-mayers-dirty-mind-lonely-heart-new-issue-of-rolling-stone-20100119.

23. Mary Eberstadt and Mary Anne Layden, *The Social Costs of Pornography: A Statement of Findings and Recommendations* (Princeton, NJ: The Witherspoon Institute, 2010).

24. C. Bale, "Sexualised Culture and Young People's Sexual Health: A Cause for Concern?" Sociology Compass, 4: 824-840.

25. "Body Image and Gender Identity." "Media Effect on Girls." September 6, 2002. National Institute on Media and the Family. January 22, 2009.

26. Ibid.

27. Kaiser Family Foundation, "Tweens, Teens and Magazines Fact Sheet" (2004). Retrieved from kff.org/entmedia/7152.cfm; Nancy Signorelli, "A Content Analysis: Reflections

of Girls in the Media," The Kaiser Family Foundation and Children Now, April 1997.

28. Lisa Duke and Peggy Kreshel, "Negotiating Femininity: Girls in Early Adolescence Read Teen Magazines," Journal of Communication Inquiry 22, No. 1 (1998), 48-72.

29. M.E. Eisenberg, D. Neumark-Sztainer, M. Story, and C. Perry, "The Role of Social Norms and Friends' Influences on Unhealthy Weight-Control Behaviors Among Adolescent Girls." Social Science and Medicine, 60 (2005): 1165-1173.

30. Carolyn J. Cavanaugh and Ray Lemberg, *Eating Disorders: A Reference Sourcebook* (Phoenix, AZ: Oryx Press, 1999).

31. The National Campaign to Prevent Teen and Unwanted Pregnancy, "Sex and Tech: Results from a Survey of Teens and Young Adults." TRU, 2008.

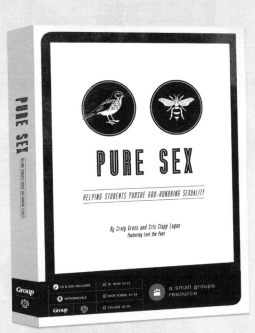